Chro

an ant

blood
moon
POETRY

Chronic(les)

Cover illustration by Kirby Moses
ISBN: 978-1-7399155-5-1
Imprint: blood moon POETRY

This book is for the women who know pain intimately, reluctantly, angrily. We hear you, we see you, we rage, grieve and laugh with you.

Chronic(les)

Note from the Editor

When our brilliant Guest Editor, Monika, came to me with the idea of
an anthology centered on women's experiences with chronic pain/illness,
I was inspired to step outside my comfort zone. Here at blood moon
POETRY, while we exist to amplify women's voices and experiences and
turn towards those harder parts we often keep hidden, pain is not something we have explicitly explored.

As a writer and poet myself, I have written extensively about my experiences as a mother, how it feels to be alive and a woman today, the
oppression we face and the range of emotions I feel about the injustices
that still rage like wildfire for women. I often flit close to the topics of
self-love, growth, the power of rest and the work we all need to do to
stay human in an often inhumane world. So, here I was, faced with
something I felt was vital for our women to write about and respond to,
yet feeling very much out of my depth. Until I got an email reminding
me about my next appointment with my osteopath, and then it hit me. I
live with chronic pain every day.

I have scoliosis. My spine has an acute 'S' bend right between my
shoulder blades. The weight of pregnancy and the carrying, bending
down, and lifting that comes afterwards have progressed my curve. I
now struggle with severe upper back and neck pain. I love yoga, but
struggle with many different poses. I take strong painkillers on bad days,
sit with a hot water bottle behind my neck on good ones—the referred
pain results in migraines that I am lucky enough to be able to treat with
acupuncture. Stress, my period, cold weather, vacumming, sitting at a
computer - all exacerbate the (sometimes agonising) pain.

How had I failed to remember my own pain? And what about the
depression and anxiety I have carried most of my life, which has
overwhelmed me periodically since having my daughter? Some days,
I have to lie down on the bath mat before I take a shower because the
whole process is just too tiring. Too hard. I read back over my work and
realised, most of my poems are drawn from a well of pain. I just hadn't
noticed its presence, woven through my words like thick red wool.

It seems, like most women, I have been trained to ignore my own body.

It's way of speaking to me about the things it struggles with. I have learnt to suppress my pain in the same way I have been oppressed out of remembering it. The quick 10 minute appointments I've had with my GP usually result in more frustration than anything else. I've routinely been told there's nothing to be done, that alternative therapies are a waste of time, and it's really not bad enough for a referral. In short, the gender health gap is real, and I - like so many women - have fallen through it.

My hope is that if you suffer from chronic illness/pain, you will pick up this book and be reminded that what you're feeling is real. The women's words we have collected here span generations, lifetimes and myriad different experiences. Rallying cries, songs, notes to themselves and loved ones—poems written to the people who have turned away from and denied their experiences. The work in this book is the deepest kind of remembering for the women who have written and those of us who will read.

When we forget our own pain, illness, and suffering, how can we turn towards the women carrying so much with so little support? What the world needs now is to see, hear and feel the ways in which women are hurting. We hope *Chronic(les)* will be a small part of that big awakening.

With thanks to the women whose poems we publish here, to Monika for her skills and expertise, Lucia for her generosity in writing the Foreword and all the women on our board for their time in helping put together this book. Proceeds donated to Women on Waves, an organisation that delivers abortion pills to anyone in the world who needs them because blood moon POETRY stands for women's right to their bodily autonomy, no matter what.

Lunar love,

Holly Ruskin
Editor-in-chief & co-founder
blood moon POETRY

Chronic(les)

Chronic(les)

Note from the Guest Editor

"Women are born with pain built in. We carry it within ourselves throughout our lives, men don't."

So says Kristen Scott Thomas's character, Belinda, in the smash hit Fleabag. Belinda is right, of course, not only due to our sex and gender but because the world as we know it utterly fails and dismisses women in pain. Whether it is because we're too young to know our bodies, too hysterical, anxious or, god forbid, sensitive to be accurate, or too old, marginalised or othered to matter, our discomfort has never been a priority in healthcare.

Research shows women are more likely to experience recurring or severe chronic pain but less likely to be treated for it. We also routinely wait longer for diagnosis; a study by Eurordis (a rare disease advocacy organisation) found that it takes men in Europe an average of 12 months to get a diagnosis of Crohn's disease, compared to 20 months for women. When it comes to EDS – a group of rare genetic conditions – men experience an average of 4 years for a diagnosis. Women experience 12.

Women are four times more likely to be diagnosed with "medically unexplained symptoms" (MUS), and despite endometriosis being the second most common gynaecological condition, affecting 1 out of every 10 people, it takes an average of 7.5 years to diagnose.

But it's not just diagnosis – misogyny, ableism, racism and sexism are baked into our healthcare systems and medical institutions, meaning we are systematically discriminated against in all aspects of medicine, compounded by additional factors like race and disability. It's why women are chronically underrepresented in clinical trials, why Disabled women are more likely to have their healthcare needs ignored, and why menopause has been ignored by GPs, despite some women experiencing it so severely, they lose their jobs or suffer a decline in their mental or physical health. It is also why Black women are five times more likely to die in childbirth than white women in the UK.

With the global backlash against reproductive rights – including here in the UK, where abortion is still in the criminal code - and the overturning of Roe vs Wade, it has been made clear that our health comes second, no matter what the consequences. Bodily autonomy – what bodily autonomy?

No matter where you look, it is clear that our pain, discomfort and experiences are rejected, under-researched, or simply not understood. We are punished for being too demanding or not demanding enough. And if we push too hard, we run the risk of being labelled unstable; to this day, women are still more likely to be unnecessarily prescribed sedatives and more likely to be sectioned under the Mental Health Act.

We cannot win.

I have known this myself, having once been chastised by a doctor for begging for pain relief needlessly and then berated by a nurse for not coming in to ask for help sooner - in the space of a single emergency room visit! The poets who have generously contributed to this anthology have known it with their stories of anger, exhaustion, grief and numbness.

Things cannot continue as they are; we know too much; we shout too loud. There are organisations like The Women's Equality Party doing great work and shouting from the balconies all the structural changes that need to take place (healthcare inequality is, after all a reflection of societal inequality), as well as the required policies to improve things drastically.

But still, what is so often forgotten is the daily reality of women who are chronically ill, Disabled or living with chronic pain, who must wake up and rebuild themselves every morning in a world that only values a body fit for labour – both in the work sense and the giving birth sense. This anthology brings what is so often lost in the discussions peppered with statistics, rhetoric and rage – women's stories. Pain is abundant between these pages, but there is also joy, humour, resilience, bitterness, clarity, frustration and an astounding amount of talent. I urge you to read each poem with care, searching for the messages curled within each stanza, because every single poem here was chosen not only for its breath-taking impact but for the words behind the lines and the water each poet carries in their veins. Their skill runs deep.

Chronic(les)

Thank you to Holly Ruskin and the wonderful women of blood moon POETRY for recognising the importance of this story, and to the wonderful Kirby Moses for your cover design and your endless patience.

Thank you also to the ferocious talent that is Lucia Osborne-Crawley for lending your wisdom to Chronic(les), and to you, the reader, for leaning into this work.

And lastly, but no less importantly, thank you to Catherine, Inés, Rebecca, Memphis, Kaila, Seethalaksmi, Beth, Chloe, JP, Romany, Jo, Mara, Jay, Mariel, Rosie, Sarah, Zahava, Flic, Kayla, Faith, F.E., Cera, Sybil, Tracy, Ebony, Stephanie, Shilo, Candi and Niharika for your craft, your time, your honesty and your courage. It is a privilege to read your words.

Monika Radojevic
Rebel Poet
Author of *Teeth in the Back of My Neck*
Full time feminist politics WEP UK
Founder @feministinvoicing
Editor @bookish_magazine

Chronic(les)

Contents

Chapter 4: singing through clenched teeth

You look okay by Ebony Gilbert
Toxicology Report by Stephanie Conn
And Anyway / And Never Mind by Shilo Niziolek
Amnaemia (sp) by Candi Martin
If I don't laugh, I'll cry so by Monika Radojevic
Bring Your Pain to Work Day by Niharika Jain

Chronic(les)

Chronic(les)

Foreword

As I write this, I am recovering from my eighth major surgery in twelve years, each another fruitless bid to exorcise my endometriosis faster than it can grow. As I write this, I am three months out from that surgery, but most days I still cannot get out of bed. Most days, the pain still grips me – endometriosis pain, surgery pain, pain from the sheer effort of lying still all these months – and the painkillers still blur me, compromising my edges until I dissolve into carelessness.

But reading these poems is the first time I have felt like myself again, and I'll tell you why. Because pain and disability are powerfully complex things, it is so rare for them to be granted the space and understanding they deserve. Because I have spent months staring at the ceiling, thinking I can feel only pain, but seeing my experience reflected in these poems, I realise, with relief, that I give myself permission to understand that it is so much more than that. It is grief, loss, mourning, relief, good humour, comfort, love, and even joy.

This is what writing about pain gives us – it gives us back a complexity that a biased and unfair system has taken from us. It gives us permission to be real and human and worthy of better care than we have been given by a system that discounts and disbelieves women's pain for the sake of convenience.

That is why I am profoundly grateful to every poet who contributed to this anthology – for showing me parts of myself and my pain that I hadn't met before, for taking up space and demanding permission to be complex when we are taught to do neither, for helping the world understand something it would rather ignore.

I am grateful for Catherine Cronin's defiance – my pain was greater than their doubt – and for Chloe Grace Laws's rage – angry at the world for making it hard for me to move around it with ease – and for Mariel Larrarte's mourning – I've tried it all and still I grieve – and for Zahava Mandelbaum's ability to distil the fear and confusion that comes with living in an unpredictable body into those two impossible questions – will you still love me if I need you / will you still love me if I don't need you – and for Ebony Gilbert's longing – she wants to go and be who she used to be – and Monika Radojevic's ability to express the thing I long to put into words most about pain, that feeling of the body being a boundary from which you cannot escape, inside which no-one can reach you – slowly folding yourself into something unreachable.

It is this, this feeling of being unreachable, that so often compounds our pain and the trauma of illness. It is this feeling that, as Susan Sontag wrote, those of us who live with pain and disability hold two passports; one to the kingdom of the sick and one to the kingdom of the well. It feels, so often, that those who live only in the kingdom of the well cannot travel between worlds, cannot reach us, cannot cross the chasm of understanding. But there is a way to reach out across that divide, to make ourselves understood and seen and real, and that is through art, and through writing. That is what each of these poets has done, and for that I am truly grateful.

I am grateful for the way Niharika Jain's beautifully encapsulated that warning, that desperate flare that our pain is always ready to send – do not forget me – because it is the same warning that we, as writers, are issuing to the world. A revolutionary act of remembering, of refusing to be ignored and forgotten.

Thank you to the brilliant Monika for bringing this collection into the world, and for everything her writing has done for me and so many others. Thank you to Holly Ruskin and all the powerfully talented people at blood moon POETRY for all the work they do to bring new and urgent writing to readers. Thank you to every poet who contributed to this moving anthology and to every reader.

I am honoured to have been able to be a part of this project.

Lucia Osborne-Crowley
Journalist, writer
Author of *I Choose Elena* and *My Body Keeps Your Secrets*

Chronic(les)

Chronic(les)

Chapter 1: the womb finds itself clenched around her neck

Chronic(les)

"Slicing Pomegranate"

by Catherine Cronin

Living with a timebomb is never a choice,
and this one was by my womb.

Pinched to the walls of robust,
most personal of malleable vessels,

concerned medics gathered to remind me
aging maternal longing might change my mind.

But my pain was greater than their doubt.
And besides, some eggs are made to be fried.

"Safer, isn't it?" I said with knowing hope.
And they nodded in sorrowful affirmation.

Good. I thought. I don't need issue.
I need to live without fearing the tide.

So, they broke the lugs off,
this trinket,
this trophy,
this vase.

Shattering carcinomic ceramics
that once gripped me to the moon.

Chronic(les)

Vestibule

by Inês Mendonça

Looking up
At the fluorescent lights,
Another doctor
Pries my legs open
Poking, prodding
Telling me nothing's wrong

Looking up
At the fluorescent lights,
I think about the searing pain
A burning knife,
Ripping through me
Over and over again.

Looking up
At the fluorescent lights,
I count the doctors
Now 5, maybe 6
Their faces a blur
Their voices a question

Looking up
At the fluorescent lights,
I think about all the months I missed
Anticipating the pain,
Rushing home, just in time
To drown myself in ice

Looking up
At the fluorescent lights,
I count the years
4, nearly 5
Without answers, without relief,
Without being believed.

Chronic(les)

Looking up
At the fluorescent lights,
I close my eyes
As another doctor closes my legs
To tell me there's nothing wrong,
It's all in my head.

Chronic(les)

Chronic(les)

Endometriosis disguised as Wolves

by Rebecca Rijsdijk

'The wolves are coming,'
I said,
but she wouldn't listen —
we were sitting on a bench
at the bus stop.

'The wolves are coming,
I saw them break free
in the basement
as they started eating
their way out.'

'There there,' she replied —
the bus was late
and then it got cancelled
and so did the next and the next
and the next.

'The wolves are coming.'

I got up and walked away.
She had bought me a tea
like she used to do
when I still went to school
with her.

'Where are you going?'
she asked.
Her voice was the first to break,
as the rest of her
slowly faded away —
cups still in hand.

How beautiful she was.

I hear the sky rumble in the distance

Chronic(les)

as I find myself sitting on the sofa
and recognise the building;
this is where the wolves
broke loose.
My palms are sweaty.
As I look up
my psychologist shoves
a box of tissues my way.

'There aren't any wolves,
are there?' I cry.
'There aren't any wolves.'
It was delirious —
I was delirious.
She nods and
the sound of thunder
is followed by rain
as I slowly wake up
and close the window.

Chronic(les)

Chronic(les)

ENDO

by Memphis Morey

Every word I say
Dismissed
All worthless to their ears
I don't understand
Why?
They refuse to listen
Knock me down at every turn
The same old lines
It's stress
You should learn to relax
It happens to all girls your age
Each word voiced without feeling
No empathy to be heard
They repeat
Each month for years
An excruciating pain
Possesses
I can't move
I can't sleep
Every ounce of my body searing
This isn't normal
I know this isn't normal
They've failed
Like so many others
And still, this goes untreated
Unresolved
They couldn't possibly
Cut open a young woman

Chronic(les)

a pregnant woman with chronic pain speaks to a male pain specialist

by Kaila Gallacher

roses are growing in my womb
the joy their movement brings me
is ineffable. but since you asked
this expansion has been harder for me
than it is for others. thorns
have been puncturing me inside
—Pain's alive and untamed; I can't sleep.
it's the fault in my collagen, hypermobility
stretches me further than I'm meant to bend.
why are you laughing at me?
my mind's getting heavier
every day, attempting
to withstand the cracks of sleep
deprivation and pain-erosion which
my unrivaled roses unintentionally cause.
they do what comes naturally. yes, I know
many women worry their roses don't
move enough, I have too
gone to triage when the void silenced her precious movement.
I was admitted to the high-risk OB unit when this pain created a void
my cognitive-functioning mirrored.
why are you laughing "pain specialist"
when you asked me to explain 'what's going on within me'.
I know my roses are meant to grow, meant
to move, but I am not your average garden.
I am made of softer soil that can't help
but give meters when all that's needed
is centimeters. my body reacts atypically.
haven't you heard of my diagnosis?
dealt with patients
like me? do you
really think
you can claim
to comprehend
this type of pain?

when this is your reaction?
and even I'm unable to withstand it?
I can't stop it from operating
to void positive sensation
when everything's pulled into
absolute blindness. and
how dare you insinuate I'm not
woman enough to be mother because
of the experience embodied in me.

Chronic(les)

Chronic(les)

My smiles are fake orgasms

by Seethalakshmi Suraj

I'm married to pain
my smiles
are fake orgasms that
Pain—my partner for life—
ever gives me
I still smile
and a secret lover finds me—
I call him Hope—
he breathes life through
my bleeds
I fall in love-
Chronically

Chronic(les)

Chapter 2: when pain is a tidal wave, the body is the shore

Chronic(les)

Shock

by Beth 'Dash' Finney

Strike fast. Suddenly, you're everywhere.
Sear down my legs, dying matchsticks.

Curl claws around my hips,
snap me like a wishbone.

Inflame my organs, force them to
jostle, bristle and gasp.

Fingernails scuttle up my spine, hang
rusty fish hooks off each vertebra.

Acid clouds haul in, and chemical
smoke fumigates my skull.

I must fold, seize into a coil.
I'm burnt, raw, withered – dying, surely.
It hurts. It hurts. It hurts. It hurts.

Chronic(les)

.

Moving

by Chloe Grace Laws

I whisper that I think my body is trying to kill me
Then realise it must be my brain because one is the commander and the
other the vessel
That might sound mad to you and it is   A little
But this lump of skin and blood and cells and hair has been working
against me
   Or working against the world for me
I've not decided yet
                Since I was little
Do you know how it feels to always have a knife turned inwards?
To feel so separate from yourself like one is an ocean and one is the land
I can't talk about body positivity
When I'm positively angry
Angry at myself for not loving a body trying its best
Angry at how hyper aware I am of every small part of me and how it
creaks and screams and bleeds and begs to be free
Angry at the world for making it hard for me to move around it with
ease

Chronic(les)

entropy

by JP Seabright

brittle limbs twitching
broken electric glitches
body causing palpitations
lasting hours even
lying completely still
darkened room curtains
drawn mind shuttered
against sound from
daughter laughing lest
exhaustion leaves me
too weak to
hold her tomorrow
tell her mummy
loves you she
hopes to be
better one day
pick you up
one day
without wincing
in pain
for
days

Entropy: the amount of energy unavailable for useful work in a system
undergoing change… a process of degeneration marked variously by
increasing degrees of uncertainty. Collins Dictionary

Chronic(les)

Quality of Life

by Romany Stott

Mornings find me frost
stiff. I creak awake and hair
snaps off on the pillow.
This isn't death.

I navigate home
c a r e f u l l y
it's all too easy to chip myself
on the edge of the cupboard.
A shard of rib shattering
on the kitchen floor.
I can hardly believe I existed
before knowing
how dangerous life is.

I suppose there's an aspect of numb.
If under this numbness
exists the pain
of lungs turning to glass.
This isn't living.

This freezing is a stress response.
The act of becoming so near transparent
most people don't see me at all.
But not always.
Not every piece of every hour.

When I describe
the perfect amount of soft
and the perfect amount of light
and the perfect amount of yellow
I mean that it is possible
to hold an edgeless day.
Even ice crystals break into colour
when the sun touches them.

Chronic(les)

Diagnosed

by Jo Bahdo

I neglected my body
since the first blood-soaked bed sheet
Now you are a woman
a fibula fracturing my pharynx
That adamant childhood ache
wish
to grow out of my body
sinking
in the crimson sky of a November rise
naked, invaded, twisted
blackened image of my insides
the denial made me asymptomatic as the sore lugged in three large bags

cut, burnt, asleep

Pressure and suppression in a periodic pill doleful and docile in a disloyal body
cream, morning and eve

Forcing heed
You are a woman

on four fissures in bas-relief
the fading proof of
a pain that spread only once named.

Chronic(les)

hi michael

by Mara Dinu

i began with a fever
low and daily from 3pm to 6pm

humans go out of date - availability: 24 hours

everything white
the walls sheets gowns people
renascentist figures not getting enough sunlight
not drinking enough water these days
my body used to host a tradition of ideas instead
of intestinal bacteria
now a tradition of wards and leds in the ceiling

we have to transfer you
but did you talk to michael he was supposed
to come pick me up

morphine for bed 8
the opposite side needs another scan
doors are slim and paid poorly
they won't hold the screams
give them something to eat
but cheese sandwiches are always gone by 6

i lived somewhere
some
some
it's okay you don't need to remember it now
some
maybe michael knows where i left my home

plastic veins out of my hands and monitors
complaining about my rhythm
faster as an air bubble is breathed into my arm
hungry elbow sucking up injections like candy
fingers scooping out my bowels

→

and transfers - new ward new surgeon new country
new bits of people

i thought he would take me home

we'll try with ice
the hemorrhage should have stopped by now

but did you talk to michael
what did he say

we are out of cheese snacks but
here's peach yogurt if you're not allergic
that's what you get when you're under surge
some

the blood has to be spit out
it will start running down the throat again

some
i can't believe michael didn't come to say hi

Chronic(les)

Chronic(les)

Just An Ordinary Day

by Jay Caldwell

It's an ordinary day

Unloading the dishwasher you bend
to gather fingerfuls of mugs when pain
slices your belly shapes your mouth
into an O of distress sends you
crumpled to the lino which you notice
absently could do with a clean.

Your stomach balloons extravagantly
like the yank of a toggle on a life jacket
like you're 9 months and ready to drop
as you sway on your hands and knees
moaning like a woman who's pushed
and pushed and "can't do it anymore".

Clinging to the kitchen cupboards
you shuffle to the medicine cabinet
gulp Tramadol and Buscopan neat
stand dizzy and discombobulated
as two overheated wheat bags
make a slow tour of the microwave.

You grab walls, chairs, doorframes
on your odyssey to the sofa, propping
yourself up, your whale of a belly draped
with heat packs like slumbering cats
until the pain slowly subsides
cortisol leaching from your body.

You wrestle with your phone
racing blackout to set an alarm
and you sleep the sleep of shock
and frustration and a pathetic sort
of gratitude that it's over except
it isn't. It's just an ordinary day.

Chronic(les)

She Wolf Cries

by Mariel Larrarte

I almost gave up. Almost.
Pain, a coarse grind resounding
in these tired boughs, I am
haunted by the ghosts of carefree
bound to a system failing me.

Worn, war torn, I am tired
of fighting the laying wolf
hiding dormant in the cells of my own personal hell.
They don't believe and so they deny
the hidden truth minute to the eye.
Cloaked beneath a pretty smile,
her teeth gnash at my tissue
battling the shadow of an invisible issue.

Take the pills, be still,
eat green, savour sleep,
I've tried it all and still I grieve
for the girl balancing on the pulse of an immune deficient trigger,
how maddening to be alive
yet see death in the mirror.

Chronic(les)

Living with Chronic Illness: a sonnet for the sick

By Rosie Watson

On the days when I have no energy, even to rest
and time drags like sandbags at my ankles.
When I really am no use to anyone
at these times, I have to redefine my value.
Not as an employee making someone else money
or a consumer getting the shiny better new newer
or even a fortified friend or delicious lover.
Rather I paint in the hue of animal, creature
hibernating in my burrow, wrapping up in safety.
Because some days I have bones made of winter
and others wind only I feel erodes the passages of my heart
and all I can do is hunker down and wait it out.

On these days I am remembering simply being here
and having the audacity to exist: That alone, is enough.

.

Chronic(les)

burning fields

by Sarah Jackson

why do you call me a warrior
and not a farmer dirt-shielded
palms upraised in exhortation
armor-plated seed a prayer a plea
from hands fluorescent with pain
I shake
dirt from the roots of every weed
but they creep back
tiny fingers digging
deep it is the nature of the beast
for knuckles to bleed without taking a punch
if I drill straight down to bone
will I find answers or just more blood
in the soil
on my teeth it means you're alive
no one wins
a battle on their knees
in a field breathing
in the carpet on the bedroom floor saints
and soldiers flee when there is no goodness left
to pull from the snapping fire
in my chest hungered jaws ready
to unmake
to shrivel the vine
but instead of burning
I water and tend
steady as the rising of hands in prayer
testing the strength of the wind

Chronic(les)

Dear Caretaker

by Zahava Rose

Will you still love me if i need you
Will you still love me if i am in pain
Will you still love me if i am feeling heavy and burdened by my unpre-
dictable energy levels
Will you still love me if i can't hold space for your feelings too
Will you still love me if i show up differently
Will you still love me if i don't have capacity to do all the fun things we
used to do
Will you still love me if sometimes we are on different frequencies
Will you still love me if i look different, if my body changes, if my skin
changes, if i smell different

Will you still love me if i experience pleasure
Will you still love me if i feel normal, even great, some days
Will you still love me if i am positive and contemplative about my heal-
ing process
Will you still love me if i find independence and empowerment in my
unpredictable journey
Will you still love me if i connect with my inner strength and agility
Will you still love me if i live with a new story of my healing, transmut-
ing past narratives of resistance to acceptance
Will you still love me if i don't ask you for things
Will you still love me if i don't need you

Chronic(les)

**Chapter 3: scream a little louder; how can we ignore you
if we cannot hear you?**

Chronic(les)

What We Are

by Flic Manning

The open crater wounds,
acid-bare and filled
the gnawing strength of teeth pressed in deep
a polite smile all they want to see

The endless journey to "not enough"
orchestrated by self-appointed heroes
Acid-bare craters deepen beneath the forced smile.

The louder you speak the more difficult you've become.
The quieter you are, the less adequate your pain.
The younger you are the less you can be trusted.
Smile and smile and smile
dig those craters deeper still.

Defined by blood and tears, instead of words and humanity.
As though bleeding prevents capability.
As though curves make every sentence a hysterical tirade.
As though emotion means ignorance.
As though daring to live within this vessel disqualifies all worth.

Let the smiles drop and words be listened to
Let care be care and not a conditional purchase
Let the raw acid be washed away by the sweet taste of living
Let the deepening be of empathy instead of craters
Let bleeding mean blood and not apathy
Let us be what we are

Chronic(les)

A Convalescent Sabbath

by Kayla Penteliuk

i wipe my mouth with brick-smeared palladian façades
catch the jam jar drippings on my apron
brush my cheeks with begonia petals
in lieu of calendula (not in season)
balance on tiptoe to collect my spoils
soil-speckled palms outstretched from web to tip
spidering flowering earthening
woman in forage
a resting dewdrop on a mushroom cap
silent.
"to taunt the disbeliever, crush one scant cup
powdered forlorn volition into some dulcet
mixture, perhaps cider or warm beer, mix
with 3 penny-weight spoons of viola odorata
and remain taciturn until well-percolated.
option to season with coltsfoot, wild carrot
or twenty-seven years of petulant ire.
note: conversion is never placebo. best of
luck convincing your patient otherwise."
they told me to take my health into my own hands
to raise them above the smoking cauldron
sneer at children upturning pink noses at wafted mugwort
collapse the cavernous chests of overzealous lovers
offer cups of embittered tonic as undiagnosed remedy
have you tried fish oil, meditation, or yoga?
no nostrums for hysterical women
i've only tried the devil's kiss.
find me stealthily plundering by night
stumbling through the brambles
coughing out the truth about my gothic imagination.
but have you ever floated on a broomstick
to the top of a high-rise
for your three-month performance review?
drink their mollifying elixir. follow the trail of breadcrumbs
to the stave of an unburning modernity.
if you can't find a broom with stiff enough bristles
then climb the ivy
or better yet
tell them to come to you.

Chronic(les)

The Nurse Tells Me That My Veins Are A Phlebotomist's Dream

by Faith Anna Morey

I know the routine. Take my shoes off, feet on the scale, back to the numbers. Walk into the cold beige room.

Answer for the 16th time that no, I do not smoke cigarettes, and no, I am sure there is no colon cancer in my family history that I am aware of, and yes, I do find it hard to sleep at night, but it is hard to tell if that is because

I am starving most days or the thoughts in my head want some company in the dark. I sit with my heart pounding inside my rib cage, a house of cards. Every thump reminds me why I am in this office. Sitting in this plastic chair, with Nurse Lori taking all my vitals. I watch the numbers climbing as my heart is pretending she is in the Daytona 500, these veins, a speedway.

When the doctor arrives, it is nothing new. Underweight. Low blood pressure. Heart rate is too high. Headaches and dizziness and passing out. The doctor tells me that I will most likely not have a "traditional" heart attack. She says it while chuckling, as if my heart is the only thing I am worried about attacking me in this body. As if every palpitation didn't bring me to my knees in worry that this breath could be my last. Embarrassing some days to say that I would rather sit at home and feel my body giving up than try to eat. I honestly would love to write about something other than this. How a three year old I know calls the Sun her friend. How honored I am that the cardinal chose our jasmine bush to build her nest in. How a dandelion has an average of 180 seeds per flower. Imagine having 180 wishes, and still wishing to be put in another body.

Chronic(les)

The Ghosts of a Thousand Larks

by F. E. Clark

Go
'Now my dear, let's not be difficult.'
You don't know me. Not ever. Not now.
'There are other people waiting, you're not the only patient here today.
Let's not be selfish, shall we?'
He talks-over–over–over—out she goes.

Jerk
Slide along the tufted grass on your belly, dry rabbit shit and ants prick-
ling your pale undersides. Breath held, heavy wood-metal in your hands.
The sights, a hole in a piece of metal at the end of the barrel, will not
still. You know you will not please him. You cannot still. At the last milli-
second, you jerk. A commotion of escape erupts where you were aiming.
He just grunts, looks skyward, peers up at the pale daytime ghost moon.
You know he can see the bird, a singing speck of black that you cannot
fathom. Spotting them is another type of sport for him.

Die
How did she know she'd stayed too long? She knows because the seven
year cycle of the gorse on the hill had marched well past its third flare of
growth. Bloom and die. Bloom and die. Bloom or die. Coconut scented
certainty. The larks, high in the blue, still sung their hearts out.

Sing
Found a job in the city, like some old song. Uprooted. Muddling
through. The larks sing high up in her head. In the supermarket in the
chill of the freezer aisle she'd hear them, on the busy streets fogged with
exhaust fumes and spiced with garlic, as she slept at night; a tinnitus of
lark-song-her own personal sound-track.

Out
'There is no medical reason.'
He was a Mr, she'd heard them whisper. He had the nurses wait five
minutes, then come to remove her.
'No reason…drugs or nothing…no-one wants to be ill…I can do noth-
ing more for you.'

Chronic(les)

After Visit Summary

by Cera Naccarato

Visual snow, afterimages, photophobia,
dancing static from an old television set,
black lace veil draped over my eyes.

Episodic "confusion, deja vu, disorientation."
Concurrent with peripheral vision loss.
I walk home through a kaleidoscope tunnel,

A fisheye lens of towering trees,
vertigo, dizziness, ocular migraine.
Unaware of triggers.

Possibly coincides with menstruation,
periods of high stress and when I'm outside,
walking in the sunlight.

"Some days it feels completely random."
Usually preceded by or followed with
"feelings of severe doom, sudden shifts into sadness."
Significant past medical history of depression with anxiety.
Bupropion XL 450mg daily.

Chronic tension-type headaches, not intractable.
Last major migraine Wednesday with Pain and aura,
Tylenol, Ibuprofen. Neither helped.
Took Benadryl to sleep.
Rizatriptan Benzoate 10mg PRN.

Multiple instances of forgetting things/
what I'm doing/what I'm saying
mid sentence/

where I am/the names of friends/what day it is/
dropping things, bumping things, tripping over nothing.
Maybe it is all in my head.
D-Amphetamine Salt Combo 10mg twice daily.

→

Chronic(les)

"Always in pain." But still able to go to school and work.
Aching, crushing, stabbing, shooting,
pulsing, writhing, throbbing, gnawing,
DVPRS scale 0 to 10, "it really depends."

BP averaging 100/60, HR 88, walking 127.
I don't faint. I stand up and walk
while the corners of the room disappear.
Vitamin D, magnesium, sodium chloride once daily.

I'm Alice down the rabbit hole falling
as I serve tables at the restaurant.
Nobody seems to notice.

(That's good. I am invisible.
Don't forget to mention how tired I am—beyond tired.
What's a word for beyond exhausted?)

Yes, *still seeing psychiatrist.*
New symptoms: *heart palpitations,*
a tugging that stops my breath,

the ice pick in my neck is back,
Pregabalin 25mg twice daily,
coat-hanger pain, stiff shoulder,
no appetite, food is unappealing,
delayed auditory processing,
myalgia, paresthesias,
numbness,

apathy.

Chronic(les)

Chronic(les)

A Glimpse of Periliminal Wellness

by Sybil Sanchez

At some point, I decided
When the diets, therapies, and supplements
Disappointed
That it isn't worth it
What it is
I am still figuring out
As I start late
Wearing yesterday's clothes
With my stuffy nose
From the coffee that is poison
And the graham crackers that are killing me softly
We all know where that fat unhappy lady is headed when she eats like that, lives like that
With her goddamned estrogen and snowballing insulin resistance
Her refusal to say her affirmations
She obviously doesn't want to get well
Because she doesn't practice having energy
Or serve up kegels with a smile
She has no tracker with which to automate her ablution
Rather, she sneers and gets grumpy
And hides under the covers
Of cheap organic cotton, not even cruelty-free
And in bad repair because they weren't made to last
Plus, the puppy chewed them up anyway
With her generic panties that are toxic despite her best attempts
Because damn, who knew that organic underwear was so expensive
And even still, despite her crack at fervor
She's unable to smugly tell of her own triumph of will
Her "Semitic genes" notwithstanding, that Holy Grail of being well
Healthy in spirit, or, at least not despicably ill
With her depraved dribble
Trickling out pee
She could never bear that piddling proudly, a nasty task
She should soldier on and optimize herself despite such sickening
But no
Without pretense of intent, she buys more pantyliners

Chronic(les)

And purchases well this time – organic at a good price
A hidden win
While she meets a quiet death of indignity upon each application
Pulling the strip off with a grimace in the bathroom
Sighing when she goes, ridiculously often
As her family chatters and prattles
With unrelenting needs and plans
A disproportionately urgent demand to witness the retelling of a children's TV show
Blocking her exit when all she wants is a clean get away
They are blind to her retreat
Each time the pee is still there and how she berates herself for it
And denies the stinging pressure in her bladder
The intimate discomfort

Relegated to a long list of too many things to fix
That she doesn't disclose
Another betrayal by this lemon of a body, the only one she's ever had
Never sick enough to stop living
Never well enough to stop healing
And the synonyms for that hateful condition which only the wretchedly initiated know: Vaginal Atrophy
Vaginal: waste, shrinkage, shriveling, waning, deterioration, decay, crumbling, degeneracy, decrepitude
The opposite of strengthening
Who wants to see that?
I often forget, but the truth is
While I still struggle to live well
And I cannot fully curate the din of dictatorial, half-baked health advice
And I have not mastered the constantly morphing needs of my chronically ill perimenopausal pissy self
And I lust for wellness even while resenting it
And I am a hot mess
And often confused
But the stipulated truth is, I do still know what matters
My estrogen belly in all her ire
Says fuck you to well-intended chirpy directives from 30-somethings
Wellness warriors who have done less battle than me
Wearing their authenticity on their sleeves
While studying how it's manufactured

Chronic(les)

Youthsplaining, redlining ambivalence
Worse, masking a bottomless bottom-line tethered by invisible strings
Airbrushing out the ugly joy of being without wellness
I cannot and will not accept this
My pain matters
Even as its value depreciates
It defines not my spirit but my sharpness
The edges I count on as I continue
Fighting the battles within and without
My pain is my defiance
I live each day healing because it's better than dying
But I will not sell my soul to do it
I cannot pretend that I am young when I feel old
Or that aging doesn't hurt in ways you only see when you get there
I will not aspire to be you
When the thing that still matters is to be me
And making that worth it
Beyond myself in this hellish periliminal time

Chronic(les)

Studying Weeds

by Tracy Dimond

I mostly think about endings, like the last firefly of summer. How the lake is drained each summer at Cacapon State Park to perfect nature. Trees are excavated, then new saplings are planted to try again. The roots must be rotting while they reach, like nerves during chronic pain.

Unavailable diagnosis. Watchful waiting. One of these fragments is considered a best practice in the treatment of endometriosis. At the root, a diagnosis is a distinctive characterization. A label without a solution while the body continues to rot.

I study dandelions that grow through a row home foundation, below a basement window. Curtains of a deep red fabric. The flower growing through concrete perseveres. The root mechanics are not my questions as the fine leaves. I ignore that they are considered a pest. There was so much joy placing them under chins while munching on clovers when my body was young and vibrant.

I study the daffodils growing along Interstate 83. March through April, they splash joy along the highway while entering or leaving Baltimore City. Imagery of life and death surround the mythology of daffodils. They are planted on graves. They are a symbol of hope for cancer patients. Endometriosis has been said to be as devastating as cancer, but it has no cure. Still, look for light. Yellow is a sign of solidarity in the endometriosis community.

I continue to study roots like sustenance will come through the words. Google brings WebMD, brings blogs, brings discussion groups, brings no solutions. Measure words, time, hindsight. X years since surgery. If I have had one debilitating period a month for more than ten years, that is over one-hundred and twenty weeks of cursing my body. More than twenty thousand hours of suffering. Factor Y for all the days of linger chronic pain, then cosign every hospital bill.

I study the backyard weeds pushing through landscape fabric. They remind me of endometrial-like tissue finding every organ in reach. Pull the weeds, spread mulch like a painkiller coursing through veins.

→

Chronic(les)

Mundane activities create normalcy. Normalcy and habit are prescribed to alleviate stress and anxiety. Gargle warm salt water to alleviate a sore throat. Pour boiling salt water on weeds to destroy the growth. The heat does not ablate the roots. Like endometriosis, excision is the only way to the source. I pour vitamins down my throat, shun gluten and dairy, curse every time the pain and fatigue creeps into my day. Wear bronzer and red lips as a costume of health.

I am still planting. Let me show you my sunflower, crumbling on a city lot. She waits for water and strains to light. She asks for nothing and screams to be heard.

Chronic(les)

Chronic(les)

Chapter 4: singing through clenched teeth

Chronic(les)

You look okay

by Ebony Gilbert

Lava poured through holes
torn in the sky
softly seared my belly
thighs
as I lay in the buttercup eiderdown bed
my newlywed
and reminisced

missed with all my heart
This woman
who used to be all fur coat
Nike kicks
red lips, inky flicks
This circuit-training
woman
workaholic
frontrunner of the fast generation
flighty and shambolic
now chronic

fatigue
slowly eating her muscles for breakfast
chased with desperate coffee
and vitamin c
this wilted woman
betrothed to pillowcase
blankspace
straining to lift her phone
when a text arrives and she wants to go
be who she used to be
so I dress her up for the show
drop her at Shoreditch station
and yeah, you know
she's wearing the kicks with the ticks

but
she
just
can't
do
it

Chronic(les)

Toxicology Report

by Stephanie Conn

A frog hops into the ward, approaches me in a tiny white coat,
springs onto the bed, says he's the consultant, gives a wink,
introduces himself with a croak, xm3jih)hg8f#ga6h!jg2j*gf9du.

I feed him dry crackers, tell him I've been painting cherry-blossom
petals onto cushioned stones and planting purple daisies in a pot,
when I'm not plucking my eyebrows with a walrus tongue.

He wonders if my head has always been full of sweetie mice,
and if their fur is white or grey or pink, and if the claws
hurt when they draw blood. He taps my veins with webbed

fingers, hoping to turn faint green to blue. He closes
his eyes, presses for the bounce, tells me he is imagining
the layer of skin removed, trusting the route back to the heart.

He hides the bruising with pond weed and tape. Whispers,
best not mention this to anyone. Outside the castle window,
hundreds of bats flap a neurotic dance under a gothic moon.

Chronic(les)

And Anyway / And Never Mind

by Shilo Niziolek

The kind of people who say / write EVERY day / aren't my kind of people / aren't spending two hours in the sun only to wake / your right brain in a vice / kind of people / did the dishes and your neck went stiff / chronic migraine kind of people / have to restrict their diet / still get sick / kind of people / three stomach disorders / afraid to be far away from their toilet / kind of people / chronically fatigued / chronically ill / chronically I'm sick of all your shit / kind of people.

And anyway / you can be rejected by journals and presses / every day / they can tell you / your work is / "full-throated, textured, out loud signing" / yet still dump you in the rejection bin / but have you ever / asked your thirteen-year-old-nephew / if he wanted to go swimming at the river with you / and he said no / for the first time / no longer the cool aunt / no longer happy to ride shotgun in your jeep / get gutted like that, my friends / fillet that fish / fry me up / I'll take / "best of luck placing this" / or "your writing is not for us" / over realizing that I'll be almost 50 / if I make it that far / by the time my nephew wants to hang out with me again.

And never mind / that when I did go to the river / niece in tow / still not yet old enough to reject me / we saw a crawdad / hawk dining on the opposite bank / mama and papa geese / two ends of a line / and the mountain water froze the blood in our bodies / my leg where there is a blood clot / throbbed / but I floated / and the two pings of email rejections I got while there / floated by / nothing like dreams matter / when my kind of people / all around me on pool noodles / effervescent / watching the crows flit over / from our bellies or our backs.

And I can't tell you / the horror that ricocheted / when my elder dog fell from the bed in her sleep / and when I touched her belly she didn't move / felt like she didn't breathe / and I yelled at my partner / "Roxy is dead! She's dead!" / but then, I flicked on the lamp / heart hammering / and she blinked her eyes / dazed on the floor wondering how she got there / my kind of people / how did we get from such great heights / back into the dirt.

Chronic(les)

So let me tell you / writers / bleeders / no / I won't follow your antiquated ideas / of creation / I must pet this dog / and remember my nephew's hugs / for surely soon those will stop too / and howl at the moon / when it rises in the sky / and nurse this rhododendron back to health / much like my body / too much sun / your dying / too much water / your dead / I must go to the bathroom thirty times today / nurse my head with an ice pack / call upon my old gods and new / turn circles / high step it out of here to make the blood flow.

My kind of people / blow bubbles / with their pool noodle / under the river water / examine a crawdad with a missing leg / scream and run from the river / yelling / today is not the day they will be eaten by a large salmon / laugh when they want to cry.

Chronic(les)

Chronic(les)

Amnaemia (sp)

by Candi Martin

1. having a harmful effect, especially in a gradual or subtle way. "the pernicious influences of the mass media"

2. Local GP Surgery,1989. Chewed biros, florescent sticky notes litter the desk. I count four hardened chewing gums under the seat of my chair. Heavy eyes squinting at a fuzzy Playbus on wall mounted TV. Tummyache. Arms and legs heavy with sweat are set to the chair.

3. Kind permed haired lady calls us in with a smile. Dr Patel- The blood tests are back, her iron's far too low. Look into this mirror, pull your eye lids down slightly. If underneath is pink, if your eyes are dark underneath, check your gums too. They shouldn't be pink like this. Your iron is too low. At home, I looked up the word in our battered OED. Read that in the past, women used to die of this, invisible.

4. A Masters degree in writing, I still can't spell amnaemia. I wonder if it is my bodies own refusal to allow it to have a name.

5. Gradual. Subtle? Falling asleep in assemblies, fainting on school steps on your period. Thirteen, standing at Superdrug mirrors, no concealer shade to cover dark circle like yours. Sleep for twelve hours, tired arms still heavy. Dizziness/ fainting when running Cross Country. Struggling to dance at school discos, the day's long enough. Overeat to make up for it, all the wrong foods. Four bags of McCoys crisps. Beef flavouring must be good for it. Crave carbs for energy, for thirty-five years. Tummyaches. At 21, pouring full bags of Spinach into disgusting smoothies. It makes no difference. Can't conceive without supplements. Faint alone in the kitchen whilst carrying your newborn. No energy to keep up with your smiling toddlers, your hormonal teens. Sex at the end of a long day. Are you joking? Give up your job. Fight with your husband. Avoid gigs unless there's seating. Stop listening to music. Your one true love. Period cycles, 21 days. Two every month. Supplements cause acute constipation. Sickness, diarrhoea. Perimenopausal.

6. MOOD SWINGS: Have you taken your iron? LETHARGY: Have you taken your iron? DEPRESSION/ANXIETY: Have you taken your iron? Fucking shut the fuck up. It doesn't make a difference.

7. Nightmares. Nightmares. Nightmares. About what is and isn't yet to come. →

Chronic(les)

If I don't laugh, I'll cry so

by Monika Radojevic

I press the body, this body, flat to the floor,
small-of-the-back push, thick ache, back of the head is wailing.
I have a mouth full of ants and I need to scream about it
but that would be one vibration too many and -
did you know
some painkillers
are administered
anally!
I'd like to make a dirty joke about it, I'd like to, I'd like to,
but mum's face - holding in tears - she's trying to tear the pain off my bones,
like stripping wallpaper,
to hold it in her hands and gulp it down instead.
I say:

Can you turn off the lights please?

Out loud, she replies:

Should I take you to the hospital?

But she means:

*Daughter do not send me away and tell me you're fine,
fine is not skin to tile, slurring words like you're newly drunk
and slowly folding yourself into something unreachable.
So, do not send me away,
should I take you to the hospital, daughter?*

I put my hand on top of hers, feel like my arm is falling off,
shake my head
and tell her the hot doctor doesn't work on Sundays so:

What's the point?

101

Chronic(les)

Ah, she doesn't like it, presses her mouth into ghost-white thinness.
I hear the crunch of grinding teeth, I don't like it, and I give her a slow,
stupid wink, hold my eye down for a little too long -
I want to put my head into a meat grinder and dissolve into
gooey strings with no nerve endings.
I tell mum she could fry me up like a burger, I wouldn't mind!
And she goes:

What do you mean?

And that's how we learn I'm in delirium,
which means the painkillers might just be pain-killing,
and mum presses her mouth to my forehead -
It feels like
she's nailing me
to a crucifix
and I nearly make a joke about it, I'd like to, I'd like to,
but she's a god-fearing woman and I fear nothing but my own skin.
So I'll make us laugh because if I don't laugh, I'll cry so
I force it, I force it:

I can't handle a whole day of being ignored in A&E mum, not again.
I promise mum, I'll let you take me if it gets worse.
You have
full power
of attorney
mum.
They can do whatever they want after they
Give me the good shit.
Could do with a boob job, look at these tiny tetas!

Mum interrupts, tells me:

Don't joke about your health! God help us.
My daughter is unhinged,
just like her father.

But there's a shadow of a smile,

like someone drew it on her and then erased it.
She runs her hands through my hair and it feels like
I'm made of water.
I close my eyes and beg my body
to become liquid and forgive me, forgive me.
Someone's shoved a balloon between
my face and my skull -
they've inflated it to the point of bursting and a part of me
wants to burst with it. This dance, it is too draining.
Mum tells me she's 'keeping eyes on me', maybe I can sleep through it?
But behind my eyelids there is a jungle burning,
heat rising in the form of tears.
They're little needles pushing at the membranes
I think, but don't say:

(This whole ordeal is only just beginning.)

My mother is a lot of things.
But she cannot put out forest fires and if I don't laugh, I'll cry so
I push it, back to the floor, chest cracked open-
I'm a self-performing surgeon!
I swallow the marrow of me
-it's the exact taste and consistency of an ashtray-
I'm doing it, I'm doing it!
I know an ending when I see one, so I keep my eyes shut when I say,

Mum, did you know
some painkillers
are administered
anally!

Chronic(les)

Bring Your Pain to Work Day

by Niharika Jain

Carry her proudly,
Introduce her to your colleagues,
Make her a cup of tea
Steady
Give her colourful post-its,
With one of the nice gel pens
so she can work on something.
Keep her busy
while you answer emails.

She shrinks and expands unexpectedly;
Cowardly at once and proud the next
depends on who walks in
through the door of your open-plan
mess of electric signals.

She knows you write about her,
how you write about shame.
She was well-behaved last evening,
She knew about this special day,
On her best behaviour,
eager to be part of your —

Ben from Finance shows you his,
she tries to relate
but it's cold and the bright light
triggers her to contort and click.

You hiss, this wasn't such a good idea after all.
She cowers, reminds you how good she was on the train
even though no one offered us a seat this morning.

Okay, be social then, smile,
at least be approachable you say
Like a roach she sits on your shoulder,
Hides behind your hair,

→

105

Chronic(les)

Simpers down, then bites your neck,
your spine seizes up —

Time for lunch,
Only four more hours to go.
Stretch your legs,
take her out for fresh air.

Forgot your pass,
Brisk walk back to your desk.
She…she's written on the post-its.
You blink, then stare at her clear script:
Do not forget,
Do not forget me.

Chronic(les)

Chronic(les)

CONTRIBUTORS

Jo Bahdo is currently living in Zürich, Switzerland. They are constantly working on ways to shape their own voice to express themselves and the home within them. They published their first collection Primary Poems in 2020.

Jay Caldwell lives at the edge of the Peak District in England with their husband and various rescue animals. Their poetry is inspired by the everyday challenges of being disabled and the nature they find on their dog walks. Their poetry has appeared in journals and anthologies in print and online.

F. E. Clark lives in Scotland. She writes, paints, and takes photographs—inspired by nature in all its forms. With a story on the best fifty British and Irish Flash Fiction 2019-2020 list, she is a Pushcart, Best of the Net, and Best Small Fictions nominee.

Stephanie Conn is a poet from Northern Ireland. She has Fibromyalgia. Her recent collection off-kilter (Doire Press, 2022) emerged from a PhD by Practice on chronic illness poetry. She is the author of Copeland's Daughter (Smith/ Doorstep, 2016), The Woman on the Other Side (Doire, 2016), and Island (Doire, 2018).

Catherine Cronin is an Irish writer. After a breast cancer diagnosis, writing became essential for coping with her new way of living. Themes of femininity, home, mortality, and hope feature in her work. She has written for Irish and Swiss stages and is currently working on her first poetry collection.

Tracy Dimond is a 2016 Baker Artist Award finalist. She is the author of four chapbooks, including: TO TRACY LIKE / TO LIKE / LIKE, I WANT YOUR TAN, Grind My Bones Into Glitter, Then Swim Through The Shimmer, and Sorry I Wrote So Many Sad Poems Today. She holds her MFA in Creative Writing & Publishing Arts from the University of Baltimore. Find her online at poetsthatsweat.com.

Mara Dinu is a dedicated scribbler of improbable situations. Her main interests are writing, film, photography, art, and petting her cat who is sadly old and grumpy. Because of slightly unexpected circumstances, she studies Genetics at UCL.

Beth 'Dash' Finney is a founding member of The Imposter Poets collective and works as an editor and writer. Formerly an editor for Oceanographic Magazine and IN London, her features have appeared in the likes of The Gentleman's Journal and Amuse. Her poetry was printed in the 2021 anthology, Secret Chords.

Kaila Gallacher - Kaila is a chronically-ill, second-generation Scottish-Canadian, mama to one who uses writing and art to explore and cope with the daily realities of living with chronic illness and trauma. Her first chapbook, mo nighean: the universe inside the comma, is forthcoming. Find her poetry on Instagram @ironrosewrites

Ebony Gilbert has the darkly raw insides of a woman standing beyond naked. She writes with a kind of sincerity that hurts and heals. Her blend of edginess and vulnerability delivers a delicate crack to the sternum where she shines a light on the beating heart beneath. Her poems are selfies. Unprocessed. No makeup. No filter.

Sarah Jackson is a writer and content repurposing strategist in the Philadelphia area. She holds a B.A. in English with a minor in journalism, and her writing has been published in LAMP Literary Magazine, The Caesura Chapbook Competition, and Atomic No. 26 zine.

Niharika Jain is a writer and bookworm. She collects stamps and enjoys painting her nails, eating chocolate, making lists and watching mystery dramas. A trustee of the Vagina Museum, she hosts their monthly book club: 'Cliterature'. She loves browsing bookshelves at libraries and watching plays.

Sybil Sanchez Kessleer continues her path as a recuperating Jewish communal professional and middle-aged immigrant seeking her place in life. A health coach and writer, she blogs about wellness on Medium at sybilsanchez.com. Sybil lives in Mexico City with her partner, daughter, and two dogs.

Mariel Larrarte is a poet and storyteller from Sydney. An advocate for healing through trauma, she is fascinated with human connections, weaving tales of love, growth and feminine power for the women's collective. On Tuesdays, you will find her crafting stories by the beach, always exploring with her two boys.

Chronic(les)

Chloe Grace Laws is a journalist and poet from London, writing for the likes of Vogue, Cosmopolitan, Refinery29, The Metro, The Times and more. Her poetry focuses on fighting misogyny, mental health, chronic health and sexuality: often through an active, and vulnerable, first-person voice. Chloe has won a BSME award for her journalism, is the founder of the feminist platform FGRLS CLUB, and was also the Guest Editor of blood moon POETRY'S collection 'Trigger Warning'.

Flic Manning was a dancer and choreographer all while living with invisible diseases. She's an Ambassador for Crohn's & Colitis Australia and Mental Health Foundation Australia. Flic, featured in Women's Health Australia magazine, is a broadcaster on 3CR, a speaker and her memoir 'Living Human' has been called "a must read".

Candi Martin is a music and nature lover from Lancashire who has always written for her own wellbeing. Recently completing an MA in Creative Writing and Wellbeing, she is starting her journey as a community wellbeing practitioner. Publication in South Bank Poetry, MONO Fiction, Bent Key Publishing and more. Find her @candi_says_

Inês Mendonça is a writer from Lisbon, with a heart left behind in London. She writes about food, culture and all things relating to women. You can find her work in places like Whetstone Journal, Digital Spy and Our Communia. She also publishes a newsletter called 'Craving Joy' where you can read about her journey with chronic pain. Find her @ inesmcreates on Instagram.

Faith Anna Morey

Memphis Morey has been writing poems and short stories for a few years, however, they feel that only recently they've found their true voice. Focusing mainly on mental illness, they've spent the past 2 years building an online presence through their Instagram - @memphis_writes_questionably. This year their poem "Friends and strangers" was published on the Feminist invoicing Instagram page, making this poem their second publication.

Cera Naccarato is a poet, retired actress and soon to be registered nurse. Inspired by a solo cross-country move, she writes about self-discovery and coming home to the body. This is her first publication.

Shilo Niziolek's cnf book, FEVER, is forthcoming from Querencia Press & her cnf chapbook, A Thousand Winters In Me, is forthcoming from Gasher Press. Her work has appeared in [PANK], Juked, Entropy, among others, and is forthcoming in Pork Belly Press, Pumpernickel House & Literary Mama.

Kayla Penteliuk is a poet, musician, and Ph.D. candidate in English Literature at McGill University in Montréal, Quebec. Her writing is inspired by her experiences with endometriosis and other chronic illnesses. Her poetry has appeared in Yolk and in media res. When she isn't reading about witches for her dissertation, you can find her writing songs, playing guitar, and cultivating her balcony garden. She is currently working on an EP, set for release sometime in late 2022.

Monika Radojevic is a half-Brazilian, half-Montenegrin award-winning poet with a debut collection called *teeth in the back of my neck* out now with Penguin Random House. She is also working on her first short story collection. Monika works for a feminist political party and in her spare time she writes, edits poetry and creative writing and runs Feminist Invoicing, a poetry project about power dynamics and what we're owed from systems of oppression.

Rebecca Rijsdijk is a carer and designer based in Eindhoven. Being born in a working-class family in the eighties, Rebecca soon realized her aspirations lay outside the factory floor. Like many creatives, she dabbled with multiple art forms at a young age. A brain aneurysm propelled her toward a career in healthcare, however. In her free time, she focuses on poetry and publishing.

Zahava Rose is an educator from New York and taught literature before her expedition experiencing ongoing neurological issues. Writing and menstrual cycle awareness are anchors on her healing journey. She is enrolled in courses with The Red School and Chalice Foundation, committed to supporting others' processes through feminine embodiment and self intimacy.

JP Seabright is a queer writer living in London. They have three pamphlets published in poetry, prose and collaborative experimental work. More of their work can be found at jpseabright.com and via Twitter @ errormessage.

Romany Stott's poems have appeared in Agenda, Rising and Astronaut, among other places. She has a life-altering neurological disorder (ME) and her writing mainly focuses on themes of illness, disability and loss. She has an MA in Creative Writing from Brunel University London, which she completed under the supervision of 2019 Booker prize-winner, Bernardine Evaristo.

Seethalakshmi prefers to introduce herself as an Indian homemaker with access to pen, poetry & peace. She is also a mother, an author and an entrepreneur. She enjoys customising poetries for gifts and her personalised poetries have found a home across the globe. Find more about her works, here: www.promisingpoetry.org

Rosie Watson is a poet and trainee Shinrin-Yoku facilitator living in Bristol, England. She has a BA in Politics and subsequently studied with Faber publishing. Rosie's writing guides her process of alchemising grief and loss into an appreciation for the magic and absurdity of life. Find her at @rosiewwrites

Chronic(les)

About blood moon POETRY

blood moon POETRY is a small indie press and a home for poetry written by women from all walks of life. Born from a desire to find and nurture talent that would otherwise go unheard, we specialise in the compilation, editing and publication of collections centred on themes of womanhood. Our bi-annual digital journal also features work from our online community of female poets, authors and illustrators from around the world. In seeking out new and undiscovered creative women, our mission is to amplify their voices to ensure we are the place where women can be heard above the noise.

Connect with us on Instagram @bloodmoonpoetrypress and
Twitter @bloodmoonpoetry
Find us and subscribe at www.bloodmoonpoetry.com

Chronic(les)

Other titles from blood moon POETRY

Faces of Womanhood Edited by Holly Ruskin

A collection of poems about womanhood written by female poets, this anthology is an exploration of what it means to be a woman. Featuring the words of 50 women, Faces of Womanhood is the journey to and from contemporary womanhood. Faces, places and ages are explored in ways unique to each woman and poet. Their work captures and (momentarily) pins down the 21st century mother, sister, wife and daughter, so that this collection can be read as a timeless study and celebration of our differing experiences. A book that draws together voices from all walks of life, Faces of Womanhood is the perfect place to meet yourself, the women you have known and are yet to discover.

This Skin I'm In by Ebony Gilbert

This Skin I'm In is a vulnerable exploration of what it means to be a woman living in a body - her body, and surviving with it through trauma, shame and addiction. A full frontal and an excavation of the soul, each poem is a love letter written by the author to herself and any woman who has ever felt the loneliness and pain of survival. They are also a declaration of tenacity and victory written by a mother, sister, friend and little girl. This is not just a collection of poems but a handbook for survivors.

Silver Hare Tales by Lauren Thomas

Silver Hare Tales is a journey through the author's family history; it's the retelling of ancestral stories and the charting of a return to her womanhood. It speaks to the idea of a woman's longing for where she came from. The lands that birthed our mother's mothers; smells and sounds just tangible as we cross the line between sleep and dream. Grounded in truth, warmth and emotion this book is a treat to heat your bones and a reminder to all women that our strength lies in being rooted.

Trigger Warning Edited by Holly Ruskin &
Guest Edited by Chloe Grace Laws

Trigger Warning is a unique collection of poems written by an array of women who have chosen to share their experiences of sexual assault and violence. Moving and incredibly powerful, each piece is cathartic. Women's experiences have been shut down and belittled for too long; these stories tell us so much about the urgent work that must be done to make every one of us feel safe. Every woman who contributed to this collection has shown vulnerability and courage - it is a rallying cry for change that all should listen to. More than a book of poems, this important publication brings out into the light what is so often left for women to carry in the darkness.

Bleed Between The Lines by Stephanie Farrell Moore
Bleed Between The Lines is a collection of period poems inspired by our inner seasons. Living cyclically is becoming increasingly important to women and people who bleed as a way of validating our unique experiences, grounding us each month and bringing us home to our bodies. With her debut collection Stephanie seeks to show us how, when we embrace our bleeding and turn towards menstruation, we are committing the ultimate act of rebellion against a patriarchy that would keep us disconnected from ourselves. Including a Foreword written by Alexandra Pope and Sjanie Hugo Wurlitzer, co-founders of Red School and co-authors of Wild Power: discover the magic of the menstrual cycle and awaken the feminine path to power, this book is your companion as you wax and wane each month, reminding you that after Winter comes Spring and so too can we find peace as bleeding beings.

All available in paperback on Amazon. To purchase visit our website www.bloodmoonpoetry.com/print

Chronic(les)

Printed in Great Britain
by Amazon

86313510R00071